# Hurri...

The rain came down.

Rain, rain, rain!

There was water
in the house.

There was water
in the yard.

The river came up.

There was water
over the land.

We went to school
in a boat.

# HORNED LIZARDS

by Elise Smith

■

illustrated by
Pamela Johnson

## Scott Foresman

Editorial Offices: Glenview, Illinois • New York, New York
Sales Offices: Reading, Massachusetts • Duluth, Georgia
Glenview, Illinois • Carrollton, Texas • Menlo Park, California

This is a horned lizard. It is five or six
inches long. It has a row of pointy spines that
look like armor on its head.

There are also rows of sharp spines on its
short, wide tail and along its flat body. It looks
like a toad. So some people call the horned
lizard a "horned toad."

Horned lizards live in deserts. Deserts are places where less than ten inches of rain falls each year. Horned lizards usually live in Arizona, New Mexico, California, and Texas. But some also live in Mexico.

Horned lizards are reptiles. Like other reptiles, their body temperature changes as the temperature of the air changes. During the day, when it is hot, the lizard's body temperature is high. At night, when the air is cooler, the horned lizard's temperature drops.

The horned lizard has adapted to the hot, dry desert. Its skin keeps in moisture. This lizard is the color of sand and rocks. When it lies still, it is hard to see! This way it can hide from other animals.

In the morning, the horned lizard warms
itself in the sun. When it has soaked up enough
heat, it looks for food.

The horned lizard eats bugs. Ants are its favorite prey. The horned lizard waits by an anthill. When the ants crawl by, the lizard grabs them with its sticky tongue.

During the hottest part of the day, the
horned lizard rests. It might choose the shade
of a bush. It might crawl under a rock. Resting
in the shade keeps the lizard from getting too hot.

Nights in the desert can be cold. Before dark, the horned lizard digs into the sand. The sand makes a warm bed. Sometimes the lizard digs down many inches. Other times, it leaves its head uncovered.

The horned lizard is sometimes prey to
other animals. When the lizard is in danger, it
protects itself in different ways. It tricks its
enemy by puffing up to look bigger. It might
also attack with its spiny armor.

Sometimes the horned lizard bursts tiny blood vessels in and around its eyes. Then it squirts blood at its enemy. The surprised enemy runs away!

Some people catch horned lizards and take them home as pets. But the horned lizard does not live long as a pet. This reptile belongs in its home — the desert.